BOTTICELLI COLORING BOOK

*Early Renaissance Masterpieces
from the Master*

ARTHUR BENJAMIN

"The world is but a canvas to our imagination."
—Henry David Thoreau

BOTTICELLI

The artist was born Alessandro di Mariano Filipepi. 'Botticelli' is a nickname, meaning 'small wine barrel'. He lived and worked mostly in Florence, and the foremost collection of his works today is in Florence, in the Uffizi Gallery. He was influenced by Fra Filipo Lippi, Antonio del Pollaiuolo and Verrocchio. As the favorite painter of the Medici family, he was known for his charming Madonnas and original mythological paintings. Under the impact of Gerolamo Savonarola's reformation, he became pious, and even burnt some of his works. Later, he gave up painting completely.

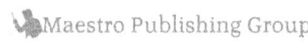

Maestro Publishing Group

Pubished by Maestro Publishing Group

Printed in the United States of America
ISBN: 978-1619494848

CONTENTS

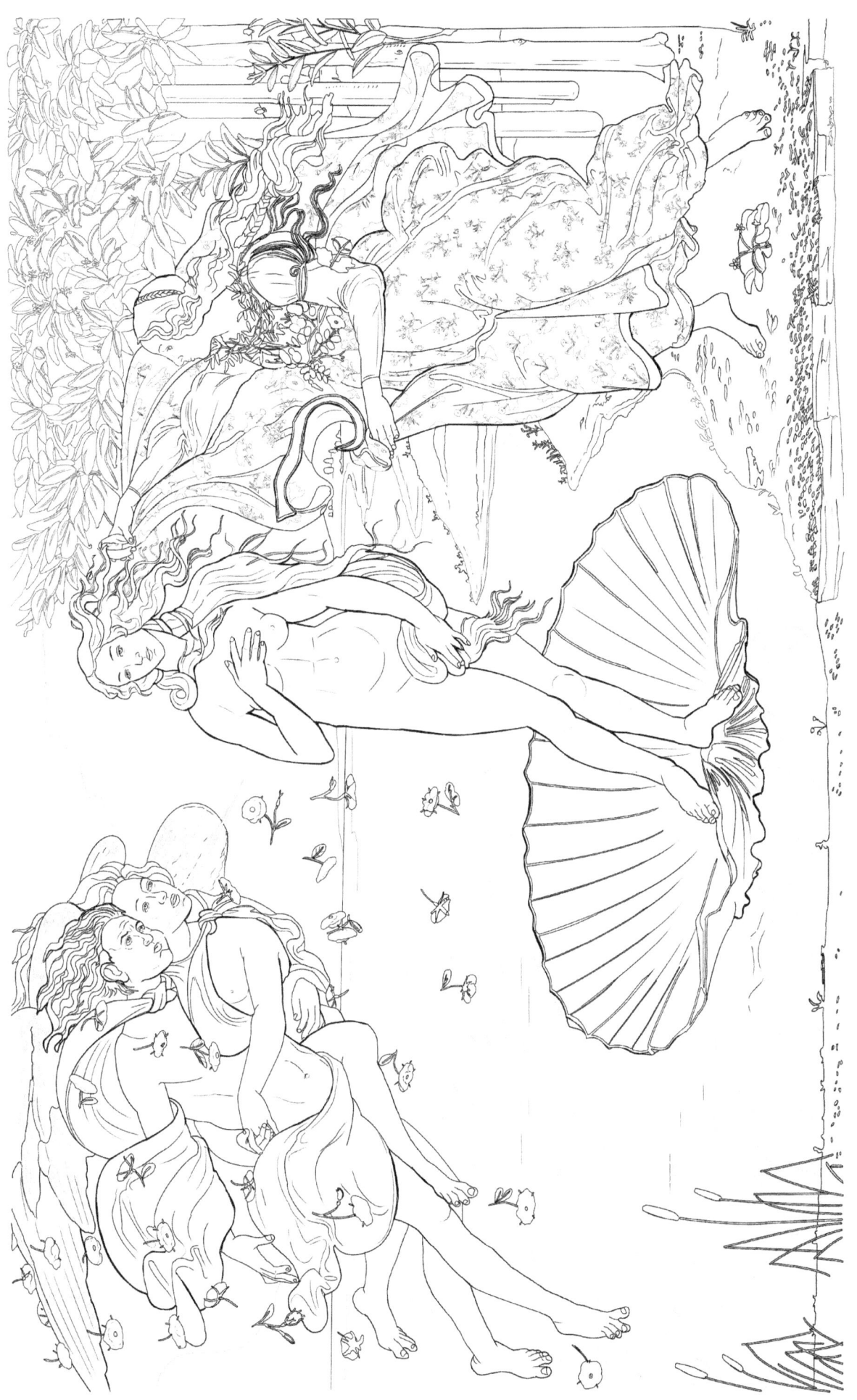

Plate 1
Sandro Botticelli:
The Birth of Venus, **between 1482 and 1485**

Botticelli's *The Birth of Venus*, today in the Uffizi Gallery in Florence, was made for the famous Medici family. It stood as a decorative panel in one of their villas together with other Botticelli paintings like *Primavera*. Strongly influenced by the intellectual circle of Neoplatonic philosophers, he painted the Roman goddess as an allegory of divine love and beauty. Findi and made an Early Renaissance masterpiece. His Venus is emerging from the sea as a monumental nude, a free-standing, gracious figure, evoking classical sculpture.

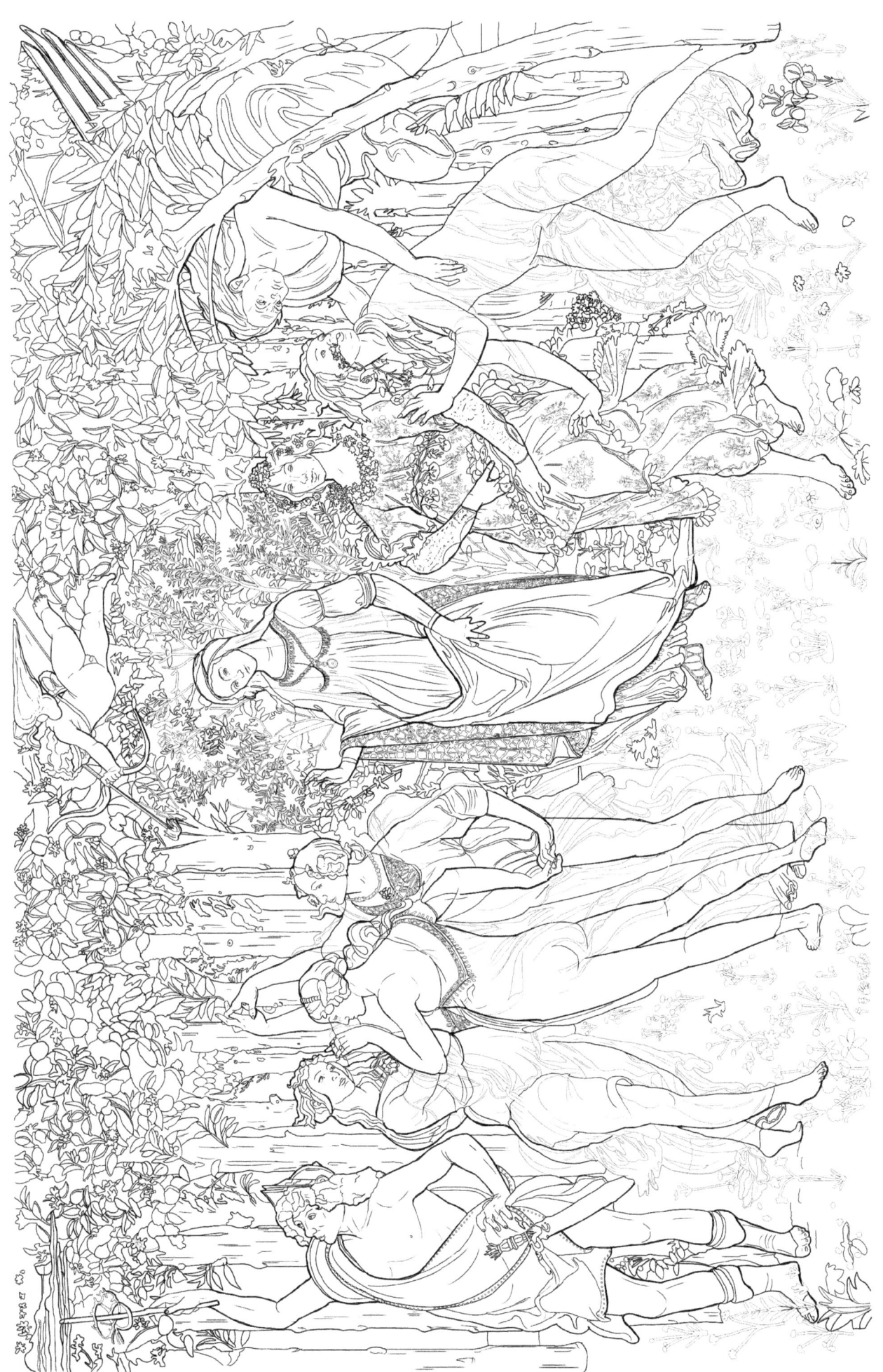

Plate 2
Primavera (Spring), between 1477 and 1482

Like *The Birth of Venus*, this painting (also in the Uffizi Gallery in Florence) is representative of Botticelli's elegant and peaceful phase. He is a master of line and drawing, and his etheric, thin bodies are floating, barely touching the ground. But, he added sophisticated colors and naturalistic details of the forest. Once again the iconography is complex and difficult to interpret. He used an allegory of spring (season) to present the harmony of Spirit and Matter, the main ambition of the Golden Age of Lorenzo the Magnificent in Florence.

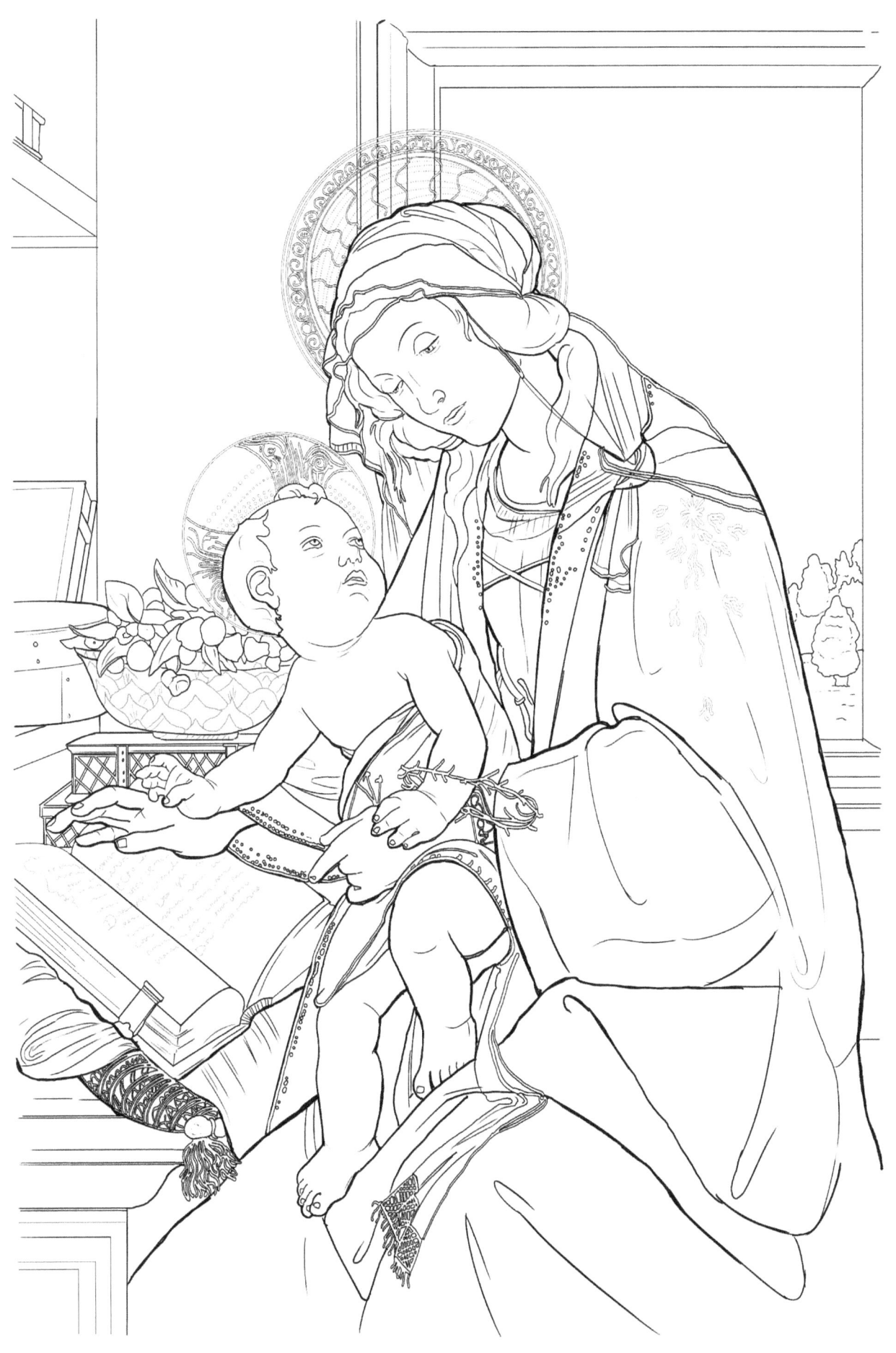

Plate 3
Madonna of the Book, around 1480-1481

Influenced by his first teacher, Fra Filippo Lippi, the artist painted the Virgin and the Child reading a book of prayers. This is a sacred image, done in Botticelli's characteristic style (soft, elegant lines, calm colors and fine composition). The details of the room are symbolic. They remind us of the Passion of Christ, and they make this domestic scene almost mystical and enigmatic. The painting is in Poldi Pezzoli Museum in Milan.

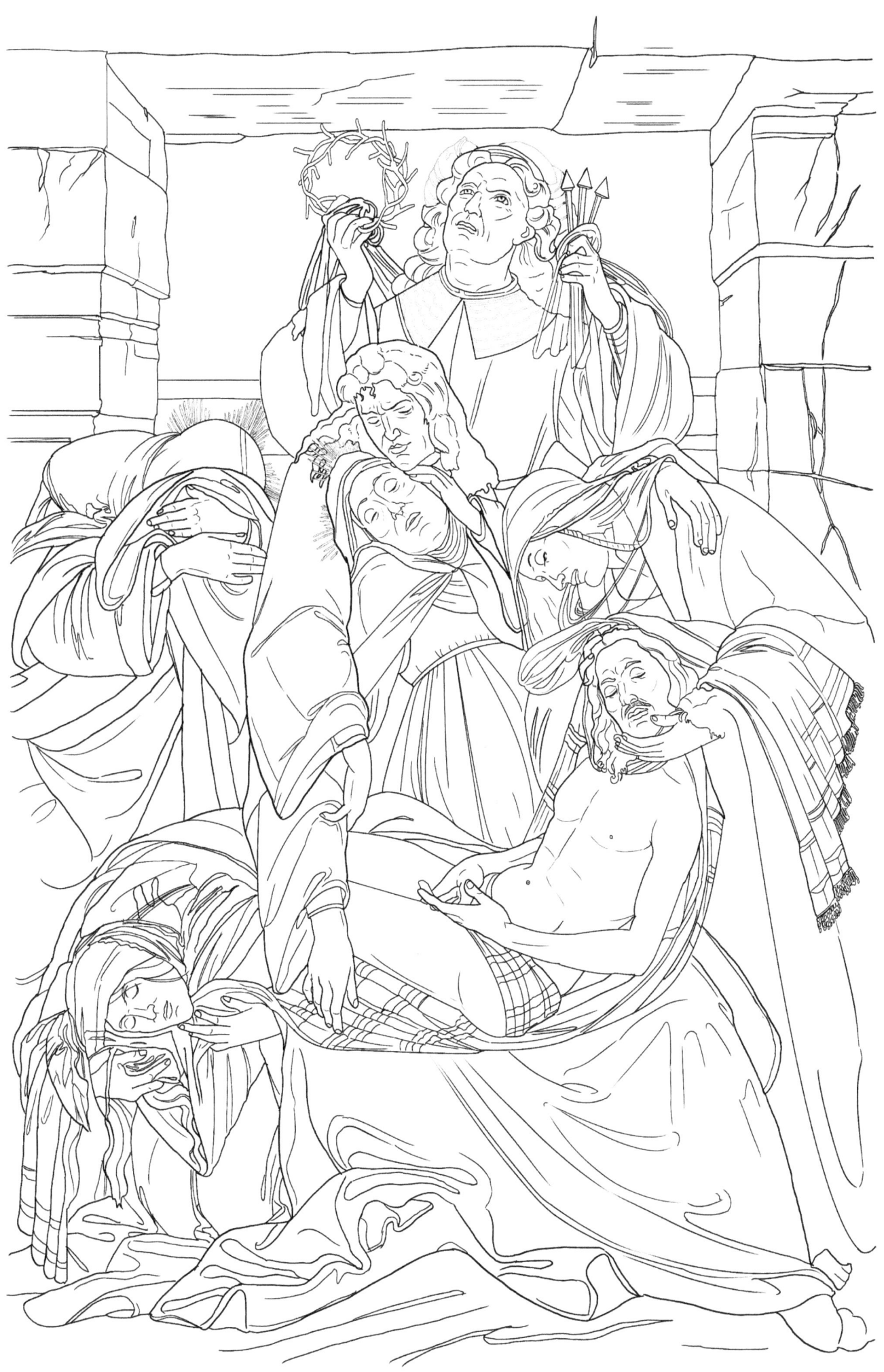

Plate 4
Lamentation over the Dead Christ (The Dead Christ Mourned),
between 1495 and 1500

This panting, today in Poldi Pezzoli Museum in Milan, shows Christ's followers and friends, mourning over his dead body. After the death of his beloved patron, Lorenzo the Magnificent, Botticelli entered a new phase. He became a supporter of a Dominican monk and a reformer, Gerolamo Savonarola. He abandoned grace and harmony of his style, and used a dramatic composition and color contrast to create a tragic, dark scene and to increase the feeling of deep sadness.

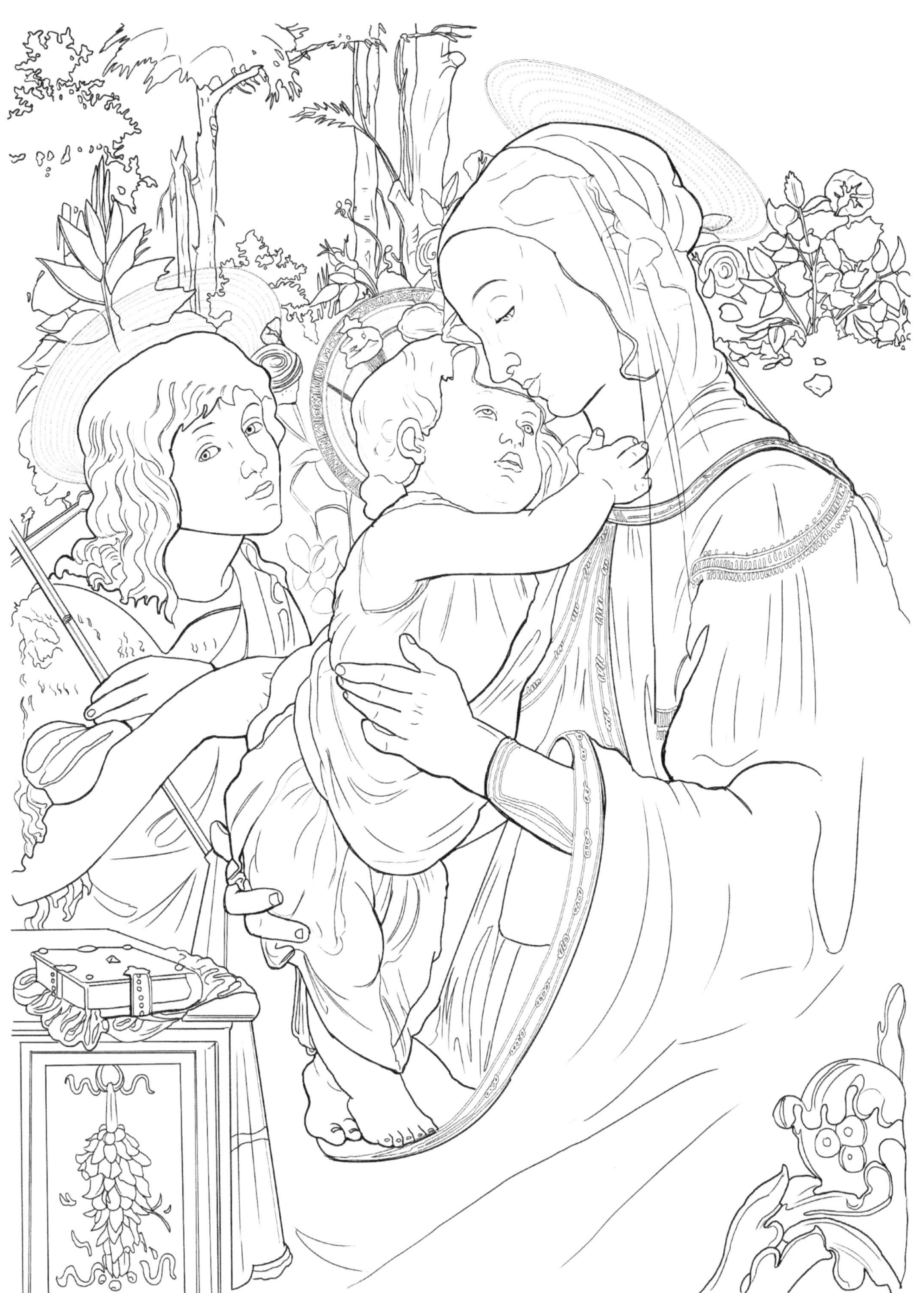

Plate 5
Madonna and the Child with St. John the Baptist, between 1470 and 1475

By 1470 Botticelli ran a large workshop in Florence, with many assistants. He produced popular compositions, repeated with variations. This Virgin and the Child theme, today in Louvre Museum (but currently not on display), is one of them. The mother and the child are depicted in the garden, accompanied by St. John the Baptist. The figures are delicate, sweet and elegant, the colors are balanced. Flowers and a book are alluding to Mary's purity and grace.

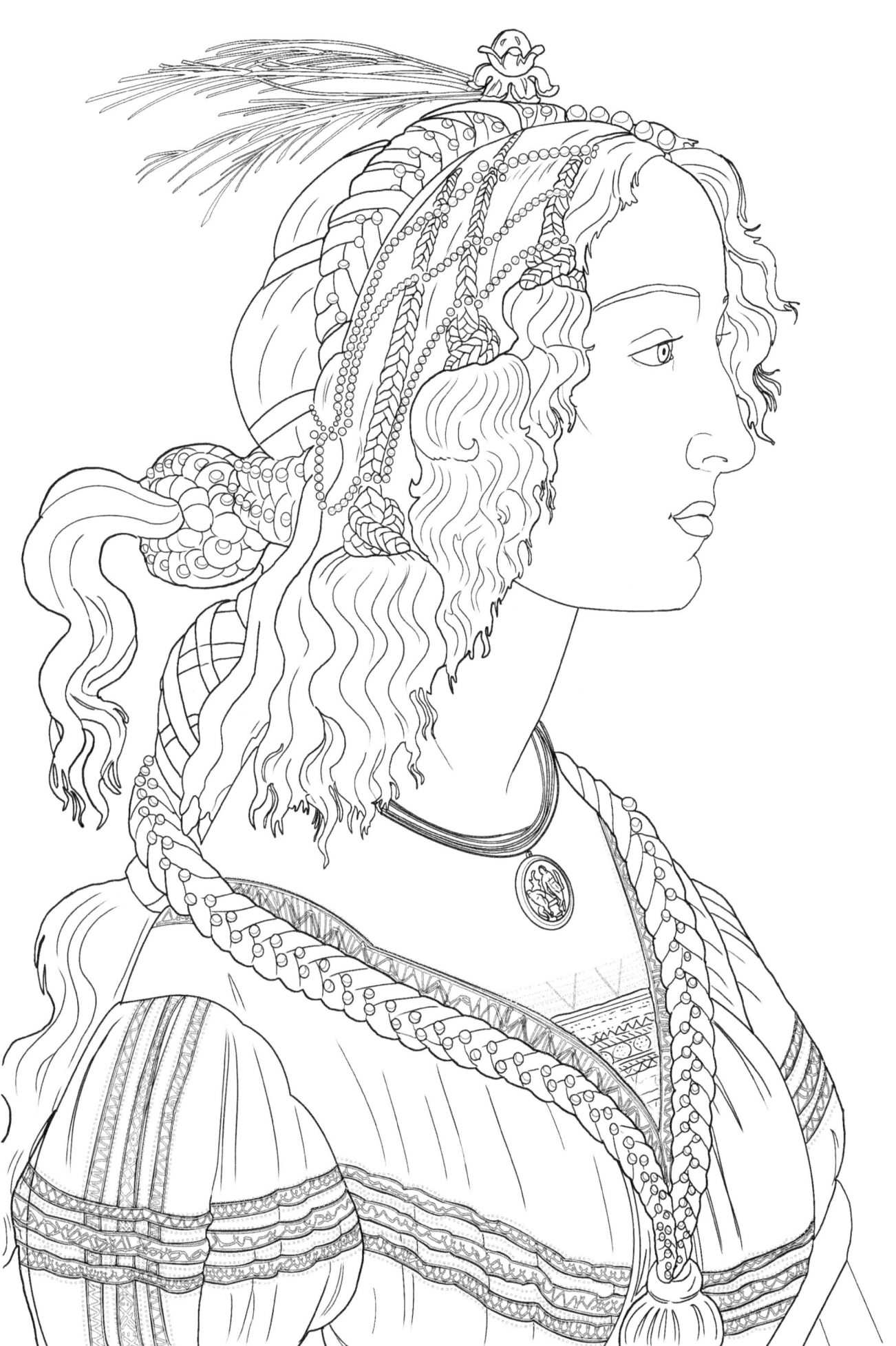

Plate 6
Portrait of a Young Woman (Idealized Portrait of a Lady;
Portrait of Simonetta Vespucci as a Nymph), **around 1475**

Scholars believe that this picture (today in Städel Museum in Frankfurt am Main) represents an idealized portrait of famous Simonetta Vespucci, a noblewoman of Botticelli's time. She was considered the most beautiful woman in Florence, who won the affection of powerful Giuliano de Medici, and died young. She was a Renaissance muse, an inspiration for many artists. The painter depicted her in a nymph costume, not in Florentine dress of her time, because he wanted to emphasize her ideal, classic beauty and virtue.

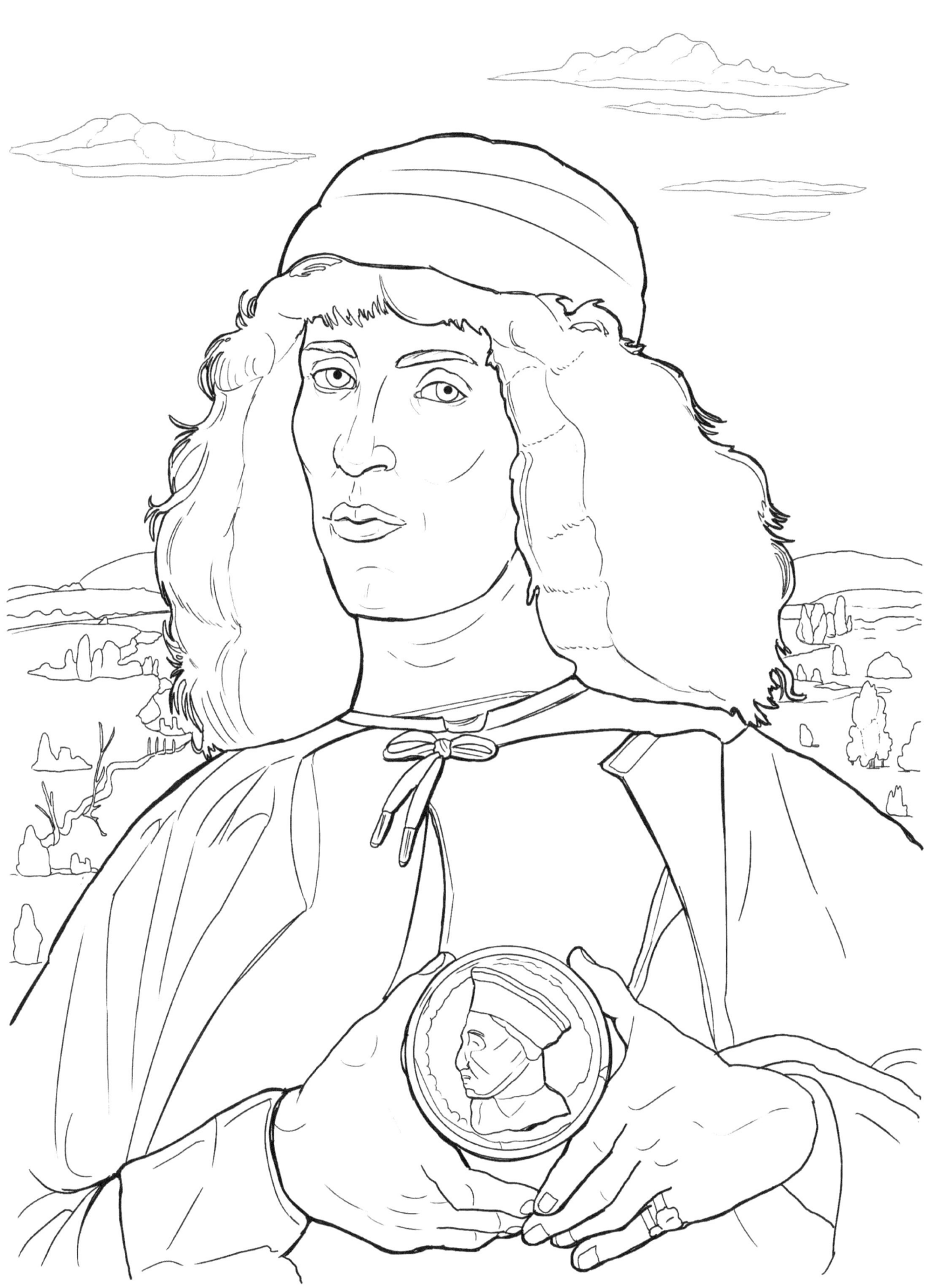

15

Plate 7
Portrait of a Man with a Medal of Cosimo the Elder (*Portrait of a Youth with a Medal*), between 1470 and 1475

The identity of the figure that Botticelli portrayed is not defined. He is a middle-class Florentine, holding a medal of Cosimo the Elder, which is a gilded plaster mold, incorporated into the panel itself. Some scholars support the theory that he is Antonio Filipepi, goldsmith and medallist, the artist's brother. Behind the sitter is a realistic landscape, which confirms the influence of Flemish artists on Botticelli. The painting is in the Uffizi Gallery in Florence.

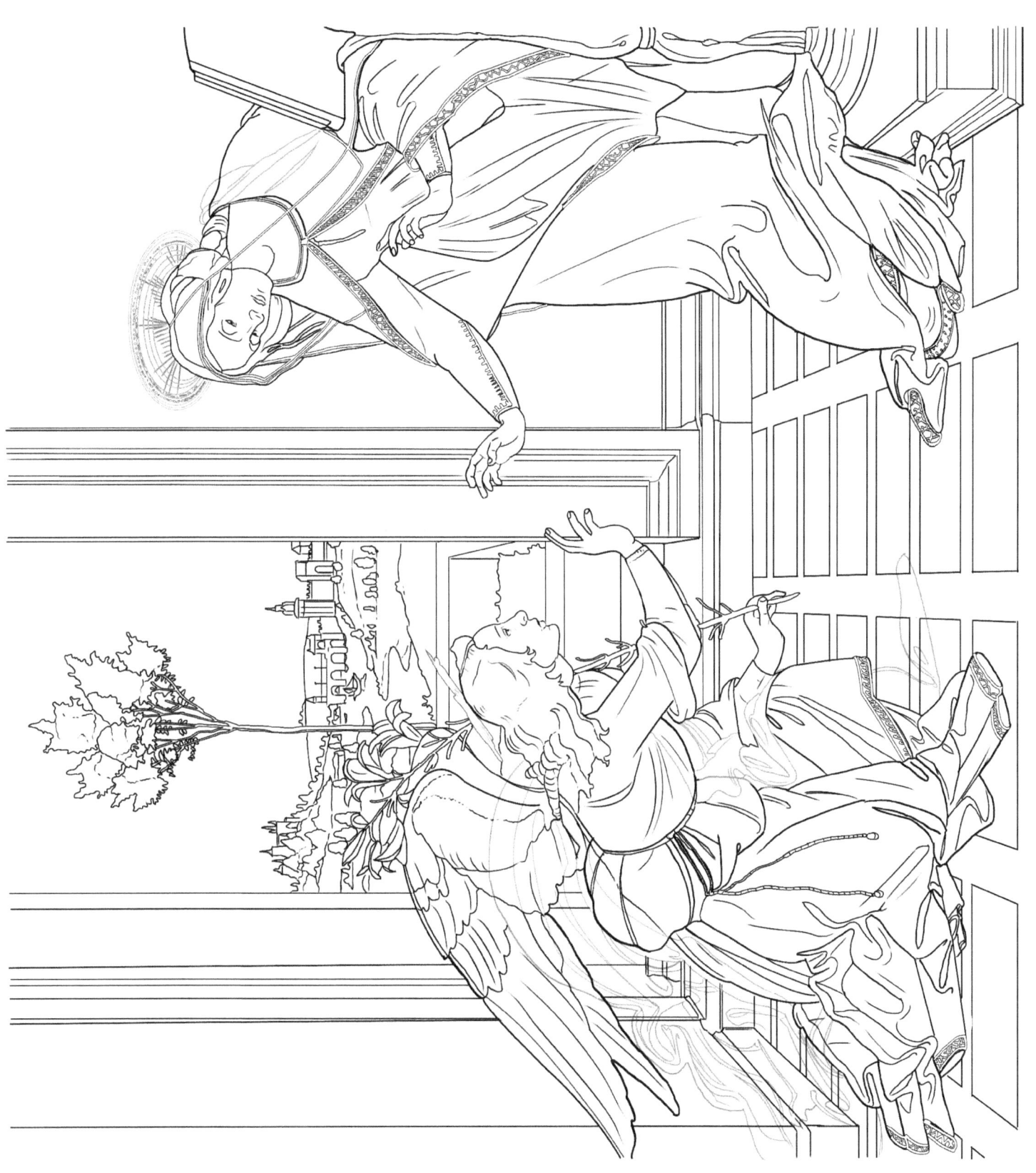

Plate 8
Cestello Annunciation, around 1489

The painting is in the Uffizi Gallery in Florence. It was commissioned for the Church of Cestello in Florence (today Santa Maria Maddalena di Pazzi). Using the laws of perspective, the artist gave us a look into Virgin's room, with a beautiful landscape behind the figures. The composition is refined, very rich in meaning, with vibrant colors and dynamic body movements. The scared, shy Virgin is almost running away from the vigorous Archangel Gabriel. The deep emotion among them indicates the acceptance of God's will.

www.ingramcontent.com/pod-product-compliance
Lightning Source LLC
Chambersburg PA
CBHW081250170526
45165CB00009B/3274